THE COMMONER QUEEN

by Kevin Fegan

Published by Playdead Press 2017

© Kevin Fegan 2017

Kevin Fegan has asserted his rights under the
Copyright, Design and Patents Act, 1988, to be
identified as the authors of this work.

A CIP catalogue record for this book is available from
the British Library.

ISBN 978-1-910067-56-7

Playdead Press
www.playdeadpress.com

Bess – the Commoner Queen was first performed at The Guildhall Theatre Derby on 28th September 2017.

CAST:

Bess	Michelle Todd
William Cavendish	Tom Dussek
William St.Loe	Matt Weyland
George Talbot, Earl of Shrewsbury	Seth Morgan
Arbella (*Singing Voice-Over*)	Emily Manley
Arbella (Dancer	Delphine du Barry

All other characters played by Michelle Todd.

CREATIVES AND CREW:

Playwright & Co-Producer	Kevin Fegan
Director & Co-Producer	Rikki Tarascas
Film Maker & Projection Design	Will Simpson
Designer	Eleanor Field
Composer	Rod Adams
Art Direction	Milan Tarascas
Costume Designer (Bess)	Florence Dempster
Puppet Maker (Arbella)	Maren Danzglock
Technical Production Manager	Kieran Jordan
Set Construction	Andy Miller & Steve Smith
Poster Design	Bryan Ledgard
BSL Sign Language Interpreter	Elvire Roberts

Film Shoot Additional Creatives and Crew:

Sound Recordist	Simon McCorry
Production Manager	Shaila Alvarez
Costume Supervisor	Susie Deadman
Hair and Wig Specialist	Maria Bird
Make-up Specialist	Emanuela Serin
Lighting	Jason Davison
Production Assistant	Paul Blackburn
First Assistant Director	Lizzy Hallam

Hardwick Hall Additional Film Shoot Team:

Make-up Artist	Kim Brown

For First Art:

Producer	Joel Stickley
Creative Director	Madeline Holmes
Communications	Gary Huddless

For Derby Live:

Bob Rushton	Programme & Venue Manager
Peter Meakin	Culture Development Manager

For Hardwick Hall and The National Trust:

Gemma Howarth	Commercial Operations Manager Hardwick Hall
Harvey Edgington	Head of Filming & Locations National Trust

Bess: the Commoner Queen was commissioned by the First Art project. First Art is part of the Creative People and Places programme, initiated and funded by Arts Council England through the National Lottery.

Big thanks to Derby LIVE for their help in realising the first production of *Bess: the Commoner Queen* at Derby's Guildhall Theatre.

Additional thanks to Andy Vjestica, Malcolm Seymour, Sandy Peet, Toni Sutton, Marie Elizabeth O'Connor, Alison Hirst Principal Librarian Local Studies Inspire, Campbell Rd Recording Studios Brighton, Armour supplied by Robin King, Pat Watson Cresswell Social Centre Manager, Julie Batten, John Tams, People Express, Rachel Thomas, Jaz Greermad at Community Enterprise Centre, Sinfin, Derby, Janet Wood, Marg Dier, Emma Doggart and Natalie Thew at Royal School of Needlework.

Cover Image by Bryan Ledgard

MICHELLE TODD | BESS

Michelle Todd is an award-winning classical soprano and actress who has been performing on prestigious stages throughout her career, from leading theatre roles in London's West End & Canada's Shaw Festival to concerts in venues including the Royal Albert Hall, Queen Elizabeth Hall, Carnegie Hall, New York, Taiwan National Concert Hall, the Canadian Music Centre, Toronto, the Edinburgh Fringe Festival & the intimacy of Handel's House. She has been invited to perform internationally as guest soloist with numerous orchestra and chamber groups in UK, France, United Arab Emirates and BBC Radio. She has performed more than forty world premieres and worked with composers as diverse as Stephen Sondheim and John Cage. Michelle was born and raised barely nine miles from Hardwick Hall and encouraged Kevin to bring Bess's extraordinary life and achievements onto the stage.
www.michelletoddsoprano.com

MATT WEYAND | WILLIAM ST.LOE

Theatre includes *Delorean* (Edinburgh Festival), *Dr Blighty* (Brighton Festival), *The Crucible* (Old Vic), *Passion Play* (Duke of Yorks, West End), *Dandy Dick* (Theatre Royal Brighton), *Porridge* (UK tour).
TV includes *EastEnders, Miranda, The Art Heist.*
Film includes *Baby Asteroid, Stone Cold.*

TOM DUSSEK | WILLIAM CAVENDISH

Tom Dussek is a busy voice-actor for TV, video games and film. Tom worked with Rikki in *One Flew Over The Cuckoo's Nest* ("Scanlon") and *The Graduate* ("Mr Braddock"). His most recent stage work includes *Glengarry Glen Ross*, *The Plain Dealer* and *Elvis 1969*. Following on from his grumpy dismembered Shakespearian head on a lamppost for Gateshead's "Enchanted Parks", Tom has relished performing another ghostly historical figure for *"Bess - The Commoner Queen"*. www.tomdussek.com

SETH MORGAN | GEORGE TALBOT

Seth Morgan is a progressive classical character actor trained at the Webber Douglas Academy. Over recent years he has specialised in playing people beset by, or in league with, supernatural / magical forces: Prospero in *The Tempest*, Cadmos in *The Bacchae* and Sgt. Major Morris in *The Monkey's Paw* at 88 London Rd Brighton. He was Abraham Van Helsing in Brief Hiatus' deeply immersive, and site-specific *Dracula* at Preston Manor. For this year's Brighton Festival he was mining a shamanic, ayahuascan seam for Rikki Tarascas' *La Llorona: The Myth of the Weeping Woman*, in Brighton's oldest building, and performing radical sociological experiments as The Brexorcist with Artslab at Spiegletent. He is currently preparing to breathe life into one of England's foremost magical figures. Also a professional musician, he has recorded two studio albums and, as a consequence of filming for *Bess: The Commoner Queen*, he is completely addicted to herring.

ELEANOR FIELD

Eleanor Field is a UK based set & costume designer. Since graduating from RADA's Postgraduate Theatre Design course in July 2011, Eleanor has worked regularly in a wide variety of styles and genres for Theatre, Opera, dance and festivals.

This has included *Man To Man* at The Mercury, Colchester and The Park Theatre, London, the UK tour of *Amateur Girl* with Fifth Word Theatre, a new translation of Brecht's *Fear And Misery* directed by Stephen Unwin, and a delightfully muddy show, *For The Little People* with Caroline Horton and China Plate at Latitude Festival. She has worked at RADA a number of times designing for their productions and in 2016 she was invited to design a set of three windows for Selfridges, London, as part of their *Shakespeare 400* celebrations. www.eleanorfielddesign.com

ROD ADAMS

Rod Adam's musical work spans several decades. In the 1990's he was known for his work in television including commercials, documentaries and drama. In particular he was responsible for the music used in dozens of advertising campaigns for well-known brands such as Kellogs and Nescafe. In particular the 1993 European launch of the Super-Nintendo games machine which was also a minor hit in the UK record charts. Since quitting the TV industry in the early 2000's, Rod returned to his roots in world music playing various instruments in Latin-American and African bands such as "Cafe con Pan" and the critically acclaimed "Afro Tallawah" where he was noted for his energetic solo playing. Rod has also combined his music and media experience with his original early career in electronic engineering, designing college courses in audio-visual technology and sound engineering. More recently he has worked in theatre with various directors including Rikki Tarascas, with whom he shares an interest in all things Latin-American and super-alternative.

RIKKI TARASCAS

Rikki Tarascas is a Fine Artist, Director, Performer and Producer. He has worked within corporate, commercial and Arts Council funded project based arenas as well as community programs. Rikki's substantial experience of site-specific theatre with Welfare State International led to his appointment as Director of Performance at The Eden Project in Cornwall, where he directed a number of site-specific shows. His production of *One Flew Over the Cuckoo's Nest* with Tanglehead Productions won The Audience Choice Award at The Brighton Fringe and transferred to the main space at The Komedia, selling out every night.

Past work ranges from stand-up to Shakespeare, Greek Tragedy, Musicals, Spectacle, Performance Art, Fashion shows and Film. He has worked in the film industry in various roles and has directed several of his own short films and music videos. He won The Alfred Hitchcock Script Award for his 16mm film *Courier* and co-produced the feature film *Carmen's Kiss*. Screenings have included Cannes, Raindance and Brighton film festivals.

Training includes: Post Grad Dip at Bournemouth Film School /The Arts Institute as writer/director. Completed the feature film development program at The National Film and Television School. Also trained with Jacques Lecoq & Philippe Gaulier, Keith Johnson and Grotowski. BA Combined Arts ,Theatre & Film University of Manchester. A qualified PGCE teacher, Rikki has taught both full and part-time 'across' arts disciplines and directed productions for a number of drama schools. He is a qualified Yoga teacher and Shiatsu practitioner. www.tarascas.co.uk

WILLIAM SIMPSON

William Simpson is a filmmaker and visual artist whose filmic abstractions appear on the stage, screen, in exhibition and beyond. He is also founder and creative director of the multi-disciplinary design practice, Omni Studio (www.omnistudio.co). His work featured in the European stage premiere of the critically acclaimed West End production of *The Kite Runner*. The show has seen two successful West End runs and two national tours across the UK. Other video design and projection credits include Rocky Das Musical *(Stuttgart, Stage Entertainment)*; Derren Brown - Miracle *(National tour)*; Theatre of Illumination *(Light Night Leeds)*, Chitty Chitty Bang Bang *(West Yorkshire Playhouse)*, Richard III and Charlie Peace *(Nottingham Playhouse)*; the award winning adaptation of Of Mice and Men by Mike Kenny *(Mind the Gap)*; Clockwork *(National Theatre)*; Mapping the City *(Slunglow)*; The Mamba *(West Yorkshire Playhouse)* and Piano Circus – Trilogies *(Kings Place)*. His work has been seen on stages including the National Theatre, Royal Festival Hall, Liverpool Everyman, Nottingham Playhouse, Birmingham Rep, York Theatre Royal, West Yorkshire Playhouse and Kings Place, London.

William's directing and film work includes the award winning film Soldiering On *(Xenoki / Channel 4)*; Jump the Fire - Melt Yourself Down *(Leaf Records)*, Anish Kapoor Flashback *(Arts Council Collection)*; Born Survivor *(BBC3)*; Its Not Over Yet – Middleman *(Universal Records)*; Talking Transformations *(World Wildlife Foundation)*; Instructions for Films *(Zoo Art Fair)* and Lear Settings, an animated film adaptation by Hull Sinfonietta's Lee Tsang.

KIERAN JORDAN

Kieran Jordan, Technical Production Manager – this bearded Dutchman originally trained as a musician, studying Music at Boston College. Found a love for composition, performance and production. After few years of touring Europe as a multi-instrumentalist, Kieran accidentally ran away with the circus... twice. Here he realised he much preferred the production side of things over performance and decided to lay down the guitar and focus on the art of the sound desk. Since then Kieran has worked across the UK with many bands and theatre productions, one of his personal favourites being "Serpentyne" a Techno Medieval Folk band from North London which helped him discover the amazing state of WIFI in castles all over the United Kingdom. Kieran currently works for Derby Live as an Events Technician and freelance as an Audio Engineer/Production Manager. Working on *BESS* has been a fantastic opportunity to work on a project where I am the only technician on such an ambitious project.

KEVIN FEGAN

Kevin Fegan is a Playwright & Poet. Kevin has written to commission over fifty original plays for a wide variety of theatre. He has four new stage plays in production in September 2017 including *"The Shed Crew"* (Red Ladder), *"Down The Line"* (Barrow Hill Roundhouse Railway Centre featuring "The Flying Scotsman") and *The Ruck* (Lawrence Batley Theatre).

Recent work includes *"Obama the Mamba"*, Curve and The Lowry (Nominated Best New Play Manchester Theatre

Awards 2012). Also for The Lowry: *"Slave"*, Feelgood Theatre 2010, followed by national tour (Winner Pete Postlethwaite Best New Play Manchester Theatre Awards 2010 and Winner Best Play or Film Human Trafficking Foundation 2011); *"Fireflies: a love story waiting to happen"* (nominated Best New Play Manchester Evening News Theatre Awards 2010); *"The Forest"* (2008) and adaptations of *"Love on the Dole"* (nominated Best Special Entertainment M.E.N. Theatre Awards 2004) and *"Oh Wot A Lovely War"* (2006). Early stage plays for Contact Theatre Manchester include *"McAlpine's Fusilier"*1988 (nominated Best New Play M.E.N Theatre Awards); *"Excess XS"* (Winner Best New Play in UK Regions Plays International 1992) and *"Strange Attractors: love in a virtual world "*, in collaboration with Granada TV (Winner Best New Play in UK Regions Plays International 1994); *"Private Times"* for The Library Theatre Manchester (nominated Best New Play M.E.N. Theatre Awards 1990) & in 1999 performed by prisoners and staff at H.M.Prison Grendon; *"Rule 43"* (Cracked Actors British prisons tour 1989 & 90, nominated Best New Play M.E.N. Theatre Awards 1989) and a community play for Moss Side/Hulme in 1993 *"Game Challenge Level 7"* (N.I.A.Centre & Contact Theatre). Large-scale site-specific work includes *"Lord Dynamite"* (co-written with John Fox), a Welfare State International production for L.I.F.T.'91; *"The Clay Man"* at Upper Campfield Market Manchester (a Manchester City of Drama 1994 production and Woolaton Park Nottingham); *"Seven-Tenths"* for Walk the Plank Theatre Ship (British tour by sea, nominated Best Special Entertainment M.E.N. Theatre Awards 1996); *"52 Degrees South"*(co-written & co-directed with Andy Farrell) at the Imperial War Museum North

(Winner of Best New Play M.E.N. Theatre Awards 2002; *"Captured Live"* (Leicester Haymarket Theatre 2004) and *"Not Much Matches Mansfield"* (Mansfield Palace Theatre 2013). Devised work includes Quarantine's award-winning *White Trash"* (Contact Theatre 2004) and *"EatEat"* (Leicester Haymarket Theatre 2003).

Plays for young people include *"Get Real"* (Blackpool Grand Theatre 2003); *"The Ghosts of Crime Lake"* (Oldham Coliseum Theatre 2005); *"When Frankenstein Came to Matlock"* (Mansfield Palace Theatre 2008); *"ABC123"* and *"The Selkie Boy"* (Ashton Group at Forum 28 Theatre Barrow 2009 & 2010) and *"Wan2tlk?"* (Liverpool Everyman Theatre 2001 and published by Methuen Drama 2008). Kevin has written several single plays for BBC Radio 4, plus a Classic Serial and a Woman's Hour serial. *"Blast"* was nominated for a Best Drama Sony Award 2001 and the stage version at Contact was a Manchester Poetry Festival Airport Commission in 2002.

He has written a few short films, including *"Dancing in The Ruins"* (in collaboration with Granada TV). He has also worked as a storyline writer for Granada TV's "Coronation St".

Kevin has published 10 books of poetry and edited over a dozen anthologies and is a regular performer of his own work.

www.kevinfegan.co.uk

CHARACTERS:

BESS

WILLIAM CAVENDISH

WILLIAM ST.LOE

GEORGE TALBOT, EARL OF SHREWSBURY

ARBELLA

MISS PENTECOST

MISS PETTICOAT

NOTE ON CAST

Bess is a one-woman show with other characters appearing on screen. All parts played by Bess, except for Cavendish, St.Loe, Shrewsbury and Arbella.

ONE: TAPESTRY

The Tower of London. 1560. Bess aged 33.

Bess is working quietly on embroidering a section of tapestry.

BESS: (*To audience*) In these troubled times,
Fortune hangs by a single thread
for those who gamble their lives at Court
to be held in good stead by Her Majesty.
A body might equally lose its head
for a life well-led as a life of sin,
for knowing who or who not to wed,
for things right said or left unsaid.
A sovereign's favour can be
as cold as a cuckold's bed,
as empty as a heart full-bled,
as untouchable as molten lead,
as ignorant as a book unread.
Beware thy next of kin,
suspect the place you're fed,
beware those who stay,
suspect those who have fled.
The careful seamstress slowly sews
her way to status, weaving
her patterns between key players, binding
each to each with pearls not sequins;
so that when the warp and weft
of Catholic and Protestant
are stretched on the rack,
she might find herself
supported by the frame
and not at the end of a noose or an axe.

She puts down her embroidery and rails at her jailors.

BESS: I'll garter my hose with thy guts, villain! Dost thou hear me?

No response

I am Lady St.Loe, wife of William St.Loe: Captain of the Queen's Guard, entrusted with ensuring the safety of Her Majesty's person at all times. I am Lady of the Privy Chamber to Her Majesty Queen Elizabeth.

No response

Bess turns back to address the audience

BESS: There's nothing quite like the subject of "marriage" to send Her Majesty into a rage. This Queen will not share her throne with any man. At Court, "who marries who" is always about "succession" – and there's nothing quite like the subject of "succession" to send Her Majesty into a rage.

I am brought to the Tower over someone else's marriage – not even mine own! Katherine wanted me to speak to the Queen on her behalf.

"Don't involve me," I said; "Tell her yersen. Thou art Lady Katherine Grey, don't thee know thou cannot do as thee wish?"

I warned her: it's an act of treason for anyone of royal blood to marry without the sovereign's consent. She knew that, the daft bogger. I told her:

And after the Queen hath refused her permission, still she guz ahead and marries in secret. What was she thinking? And now, with child – God save us. Small wonder Her Majesty is furious. The girl hath nothing short of a death-wish. Well, she can wing her own way to the block; I will not accompany her on that particular dance.

Hath she learned nothing from the execution of her gentle sister, Lady Jane? I keep her portrait, still, by my bedside.

William St.Loe appears on the screen.

ST.LOE: (*Calling*) Bess! Bess! They will not let me see thee.

BESS: Mine own dearest Will.

ST.LOE: Mine own, more dear to me than I am to myself; tell me thou art well?

BESS: I pass the time: they hath left me with my embroidery; but they hath also left me with my thoughts.

ST.LOE: Do not forsake. I hath spoken to Sir Edward. He will question thee soon, and with great respect, or he shall answer to me.

BESS: How can Her Majesty doubt me? Speak to Her Majesty, Will; tell her of my innocence.

17

She will listen to thee. Did you not spend time together within these walls, with the Princess Elizabeth?

ST.LOE: At that time there were those who would die to have her as their sovereign in place of her sister, the bloody Queen Mary. I would never implicate the Princess Elizabeth. I held my tongue, despite their threats to tear it from my mouth.

BESS: Her Majesty owes thee her life.

ST.LOE: The Queen knows only too well the terrors of The Tower. She begged for a sword and not the axe, as befell her own sweet mother, Anne Boleyn.

BESS: Go; beseech her. Her Majesty favours us both. She knows us for the loyal servants that we are. She cannot choose to believe I would encourage the wilful Katherine in her treason.

St.Loe disappears. Bess turns back to the audience.

Seems to me that every person of note
at Court is one time sent to The Tower.
'Tis true that many end up on the block,
in a show of power; but others are released.
I hath not come this far to have my head
displayed for all to see and mock,
as though it were a stage prop
in some base London theatrical.

St. Loe re-appears on screen.

BESS: Fortunately for me,
my knight in shining armour
fills the Queen with admiration
and fills me with his amour
when he rides in with a royal pardon
and rides out with me on horse.

Music

TWO: THE COMMON QUEEN

Chatsworth House. 1570. Bess aged 43. Mary Queen of Scots aged 28. Queen Elizabeth aged 37.

BESS: (*To audience*) A queen must assert the power
given to her by God;
it is her duty to rule
her subjects and not spare the rod.
A sovereign is the spool
on which the country turns:
at times providing slack for her subjects
to expand and invest
and, other times, winding in their excess.
Our dearest Queen Elizabeth hath overseen
an age of expansion
into the New World
and defeated the Spaniards;
in commerce and science, theatre and fashion,
we have excelled;
but our great monarch hath held fast
against the forces of chaos and rebellion.
Such hath been my rich life at Court
that I hath oft-times wrought from jail to jailor
in a single stitch of the needle.
With my fourth and final husband, George Talbot,
Earl of Shrewsbury,
we find ourselves especially favoured
by the Queen to "house" her papist cousin,
the Scottish Queen, Mary Stuart;

to care for her every need
except, of course, the need to escape.
Many an hour hath we enjoyed
each other's company
in the gentle art of embroidery.

Bess takes up her embroidery with Mary Queen of Scots

BESS: (*To Mary Queen of Scots*) Your Royal
Highness hath great talent as a seamstress.

(*As Mary*) You must call me "Mary" – "Mary
Stuart, Queen of Scotland and France. And
maybe one day, Angleterre.

(*Aside*) A queen without a country. A Scot
with a French accent.

(*As Mary*) And I must call you "Bess", my
lady. This Chatsworth House of yours, je
t'aime beaucoup. An habitation fit for a
queen. Your Castle Tutbury was like the
dungeon for criminals. The garden for
exercise was a potato patch fit only for the
pigs.

(*Aside*) I ask if there's anything we can
provide to improve her stay?

(*As Mary*) I have a grief of the spleen. Peut-
etre, you arrange for me to visit your famous
spa water?

21

(*Aside*) Aye up, tell thee what, it'ld be a darn sight cheaper than her bathing in white wine at our expense.

(*As Mary*) I require a cloth of state upon my chair... and pigeons.

(*To Mary*) Pigeons? For the table?

(*As Mary*) Non. As pets.

(*Aside*) Pigeons? Methinks the cunning of which Lord Burghley warns may yet be true. I reassure Her Highness we are forever her humble servants, but we too are at the mercy of our queen.

(*As Mary*) You must invite your queen to enjoy Chatsworth for herself.

(*To Mary*) When the building is complete, it is my sincere hope Her Majesty will indeed visit.

(*Aside*) She knows we're both desperate for a royal visit. I'd dearly love to show off my beloved Chatsworth; Mary, of course, to argue for her freedom.

(*As Mary*) Does your queen ask of me?

(*To Mary*) She enquires about thine appearance.

(*As Mary*) How so?

Bess recalls her conversation with Queen Elizabeth.

The Queen asketh me, straight: "My dearest Bess, who is the higher?"

I said, "Your Majesty, I am thy humble servant."

"Yes, yes, but who is the higher?"

So I told her: "She is, my liege."

"Then she is too high."

(*As Mary*) I will send her my portrait and a looking glass, that she may see also who is the fairest.

(*Aside*) Who could have thought this Derbyshire lass would one day be tab-hanging between two great queens?

(*As Mary*) What if I send her this embroidery of mine? It is a vine. On one side it is laden with fruit; the other, it is barren.

(*To Mary*) There are those who sayeth that barrenness is the best blossom of beauty.

(*As Mary*) Mais oui, I have heard my cousin is seduced by flattery.

(*To Mary*) Her Majesty is still of child-bearing age.

(*As Mary*) They say she is not like other women. What say you? You have seen her in her bedchambre?

(*To Mary*) Perhaps thou should ask Lord Leicester?

(*As Mary*) Ah, my lady Bess, if only Elizabeth were a man, we might have married and resolved our difficulties.

(*To Mary*) Her Majesty's husband is the kingdom of England.

(*As Mary*) But can a kingdom satisfy a woman?

And you, Lady Bess, what of your husbands?

(*To Mary*) These images I sew, they are symbols of husbands past: the lamb is Robert, my sweet child husband; the bear is William Cavendish, my rock and father of my children; and the stag is Captain St.Loe, my knight in shining armour.

(*As Mary*) My first amour also was a sweet and sickly child, but he made me Queen of France. The second was the father of my child, but he was a great cock-chick and a drunken brute who deserved his fate at the hands of my third – Lord Bothwell. Now there was a man; I would have followed him to the end of the world in my petticoat.

(*Aside*) Some women would do well to forsake a husband. Our Virgin Queen might yet prove wiser than we know.

(*As Mary*) I return from France to be their Queen and the Scottish lords threaten to slit my throat and force me to abdicate. Maintenant, my son James is estranged and they groom the boy king against his own mother – (*considering Bess' embroidery*) and these? What are these?

(*To Mary*) Tears, Your Grace: a tear for each and every husband past.

(*As Mary*) And what of your husband present – your Earl of Shrewsbury? Will this also end in tears?

(*Aside*) I ask what feelings she has for the Duke of Norfolk, who hath lost all to be her suitor?

(*As Mary*) I cannot answer for every Catholic who would have me as their queen. Norfolk must answer for himself.

(*Aside*) I'm afeared it'll all come out in t'wash. I tell her I'll try and put in a good word for her to mine husband.

Music. Shrewsbury appears on screen.

SHREWSBURY: Who are all these damned people? What are they doing here?

BESS: They've come to see me.

SHREWSBURY: How so?

BESS: George, just announce yersen in the courtly manner.

SHREWSBURY: At whose court?

BESS: Mine, George. You're in my story.

SHREWSBURY: So-be-it.

(*To Audience*) George Talbot, Earl of Shrewsbury – her husband.

BESS: Number Four.

SHREWSBURY: (*To Audience*) "Countess of Shrewsbury", how she loves that title. She knew what she was doing when she went fishing for me: marrying into the aristocracy. Do not mistake, the old girl was a welcome catch in my older years; and she did come with a shilling or two, several houses and a few plots of land. Humble beginnings, I know, but our families hath known each other for years – I was already Godfather to one of her brood. And we were neighbours, what with me down the highway at Sheffield Castle. One cannot afford to ignore "new money" these days. Smart move tying the families together in wedlock: her eldest Henry and my girl Grace; my son Gilbert and her Mary. A sort of triple family betrothal; all done in one go. Keep the paperwork simple. Bravo. And to cap it all, Bess is known to be the Queen's favourite.

Of course, I am also favoured by Her Majesty – this time to preside over Norfolk's treason. Decent enough fellow, Norfolk, for a papist; but I'm afraid the offences are plain for all to see. He will have his trial, but there is no doubting the outcome. Damn fool. Let me be the first to admit, this Scottish Queen hath her charm and allure; I myself hath fallen for it on occasions, with that damn horny accent of hers. Good horsewoman too, splendid ride. But therein lies the folly.

These Catholics are the enemy of the state. The pope instructs them to rise up and depose our blessed sovereign. We hath had one bloody Queen Mary, we certainly do not want another in a hurry. And we certainly do not want the French or the Spaniards thinking they can slip in through the back door.

I suppose with Norfolk out of the way, the Shrewsburys will be the highest ranking peers of the realm? That should keep her happy, up at Chatsworth.

It is costing me a damn fortune, looking after this Scottish-French pretender. Her Majesty is grateful, of course; we have it in writing: "My debt to you is as great as a sovereign can owe a subject". One continues to ask Lord Burghley to have a word; a little subsidy would not go amiss. And now this horrible business with Norfolk. Turning out to be a bit of a poisoned chalice. It was I who found her coded letters to Norfolk and sent them off to Burghley. And yet Her Majesty is angry with me! Damned unfair, I say. It will all end in tears, mark my words.

Music

THREE: RAISING A PRINCESS

Chatsworth. 1590. Bess aged 63.

Bess prepares Arbella for court. Arbella is represented by a puppet doll, controlled by Bess.

BESS: (*To Arbella*) My little jewel, we need to find thee an husband. Not any random husband, but one fit for a princess royale. Thou's fifteen years now, Arbella, and of marriageable age. I was married since at thine age and widowed one year later. I know thou's been to Court afore, but 'appen this time it will be different. Whilst ever Shrewsbury was alive, all that I owned was his. Now the "mad dog" hath been laid to rest, I find mesen the richest woman in the land – notwithstanding Her Royal Highness, of course – with 37 manors, 400,000 acres of land and the finest collection of tapestries. I shall teach thee about sheep and cattle farming, property rentals and leaseholds, quarries, mines and foundries. I shall teach thee about money-lending and securing loans with mortgages and the joys of building. It is my intention to build us a new home at Hardwick and the New Hall shall be fit for a queen. I might be a beldam, four times widowed and in her sixth decade, but still I plot great ambitions for me and mine.

Our sojourn to Court shall be like a Royal Progress. We shall travel down as a family in

separate coaches with 40 servants and 43
horse. I shall have 12 waggons of luggage –
the rest I shall send ahead. We shall stop
along the way for 7 nights and be sure to
give 40 shillings to the poor of the town at
every stop.

In London, we shall stay at Shrewsbury
House, our residence in Chelsea, looking over
The Thames, where we shall entertain like
royalty. I shall summon tailors to make us
suitable wardrobes for Court and a gown for
the Queen as a New Year gift. The capital
shall have witnessed nothing the like, since
the last state visit. We shall go shopping:
royal fur for thee and furnishings for the
New Hall.

Thou won't remember thy fether – like mine
own, thou were but an infant when he died.
Me and thy grandmama Lennox, we knew it
was a risk when we introduced thy parents,
without seeking the Queen's permission; but
thou should know they married for love. Thy
fether was a Stuart, as ye know, of royal
blood. All hell broke loose at thy birth. The
Queen was furious.

Grandmama Lennox was arrested and I was
taken to the Tower for questioning. George
had to plead with the Queen for our safety.

Thy cousin James is King of Scotland and
first-in-line to the throne of England. Thine

Aunt Mary, God rest her soul, was second-in-line, but, since her execution, second-in-line falls to thee. Her Majesty started out third-in-line line, just like thee; then second, then look what happened? What if something should happen to James? There's always those who'll plot to crown thee for their own political gains, remember that, Arbell. Listen to thy grandma Bess, she knoweth best. Aye, tha's some pedigree, lass. My little jewel is a proper princess.

Thou resemble thy mother in looks, Arbell. Dust thou remember her? Thou were but six or seven when I lost my young, sweet Elizabeth. There is a long line of Elizabeths in our family – 'appen why I ended up "Bess". She made me promise to take care of her "little innocent". I asked Her Majesty for permission to adopt thee. Dust remember thou wrote me, "My good lady grandmother", and sent me clippings of thine hair and a pot of jam? We still had thine Aunt Mary, the Scottish Queen, living with us, but my plans were always with thee. I encouraged George to service Mary, as far as possible, whilst I set-to with caring for thee.

Now, the Duke of Palma hath requested a portrait of my little jewel. The Spanish Ambassador shall be at Court to meet us. Thee could find theesen crowned Queen of Spain afore long. Wouldst that pleaseth

Arbell? For certes, it would not please Her
Majesty, who will not risk her crown falling
into Spanish hands.

Music

FOUR: FAMILY

1546 – 1557. Bess aged 19 – 30.

Bess is in service at the home of Lord and Lady Grey.

BESS: Fether left me forty marks in his will
to make mesen a fortune,
whenever I was ready to leave home
and weave my life upon the loom.
I was a babe in arms when fether died.
Mam kept her five young children
close to her bedside.
On the bedstead, she hung a holey stone
on a black cotton thread
to ward off nightmares of the unknown.
A widow is not allowed
to keep her husband's estate,
most of which is taken by the Crown.
So mam re-married
that we might keep our home,
the manor house at Hardwicke,
where our family hath lived for two
centuries.
She taught us letters and arithmetic,
and woman's work:
baking and gardening,
washing, cleaning and polishing,
spinning and weaving,
poultry and bee-keeping,
how to be the perfect waitress
and an accomplished seamstress,
which mam believed, give a girl status.

We played in the gardens with dolls and
models,
sling-shots and spinning-tops,
bows and arrows,
hide-and-seek and leap-frog.
Age twelve, as a little miss,
I took my forty marks
and was sent into service
for Lady Zouche, where I was betrothed
to the gentle and sickly Robert Barlow.
We were but children,
dressing up in married clothes;
I was a bride of restricted years,
tending as a nurse at his bedside
until my little lamb, Robert, died.
I was sent to the great city of London
to wait upon Lady Frances Grey,
where I learned how to dance
and play the virginals and was taught
all about fashion and furnishings,
to prepare me for a life at Court.
Lord Cavendish, a close friend of Henry
Grey,
spent many a day with us, hunting and
gambling;
and I must say, the attention paid
to me by Sir William Cavendish
left me feeling rather flushed and foolish.

Music. Bess takes up her household duties.

BESS: (*To Audience*) This is me, age 19, in service at the home of Lord and Lady Henry and Frances Grey.

Cavendish appears on screen.

BESS: Not now, Cavendish. I'll call you up when I'm good and ready. (*Aside*) Honestly, whose story do they think it is? I have an important speech to deliver first.

(*Clearing her throat*) A woman's place is to serve; I know this. As a girl, it is to serve her parents and bring no shame unto the good family name. Then, to serve in a fine lady's home and learn to run a household.

As a woman, it is to serve her husband: to keep a good house and a warm bed for him that he might provide for his family.

As a mother, it is to serve her children, that they might grow up decent and use their talents wisely.

As a loyal subject, it is to serve her sovereign and defend their divine right to rule.

As a pious creature of this world, it is to serve her God in good faith, that He might guide her to heaven and a life everlasting in the glory of His name.

(*To Cavendish*) All reight, now thou canst appear and announce theesen.

CAVENDISH: Sir William Cavendish, at thy service.

BESS: Good. Thou canst proceed to "woo" me.

CAVENDISH: (*To Audience*) Not a great beauty, it hath to be said; but regular, attractive features, with an alert, intelligent expression. Slender, upright carriage; well-shaped hands - always a good sign of breeding. Sharp blue eyes and flaming red hair, all curls, probably a bit fiery.

BESS: (*To Audience*) I know he's twice my age; but it's only numbers after all. He's a great, big, corpulent bear of a man; but a good belly on a man is a sign of wealth and fine living. Treasurer of the King's Chamber – I like a man with a head for figures. Made his wealth from the dissolution of the monasteries. We're both followers of the new reformed religion and pray from the new Common Book of Prayer.

CAVENDISH: (*To Audience*) I must say, Lady Frances hath done a splendid job training her up, ready for a life at Court. A young widow, apparently? Widowed twice myself, don't you know? Wives keep dying on me. Still a virgin, by all accounts – damn sure I could help her out there.

BESS: (*To Audience*) Will he be tender in the bedchamber? Will he show me how to proceed? He is a man of great experience.

Though I have loved, I hath not yet known a man. Would that Robert had lived, that I might have borne him children. I do hope for love. At the very least, status and protection. A provider who can shield me from the vagaries of life. Is this how mam felt when fether died? Why should I be forced to fight in the courts for what's rightfully mine? Mam re-married. If I'm not to eat horse-corn for the rest of my days, I must do the same.

CAVENDISH: (*To Audience*) Henry tells me she never knew her father. Henry also tells me I present myself rather well as a father-figure. Bess is good with the children by all accounts – Lady Jane follows her around like a bear cub.

BESS: (*To Audience*) William hath three daughters – the eldest is but seven years short of mine own age – and he hath at least two fine houses. It is indeed much for a woman of nineteen years to take on, but I shall take charge of his household and turn it to our advantage.

CAVENDISH: (*To Audience*) Despite her lowly standing, it seems she hath a good lineage – her roots go all the way back to Edward I, don't you know?

BESS: (*To Audience*) I shall marry this William Cavendish and I shall bear him many children. I shall learn to love him and stand by him in all things. I shall be "Lady Cavendish" and restore the good name of the Hardwickes. I shall make fether proud and return us to former glories.

CAVENDISH: (*To Bess*) Good Bess, I am a simple Accountant; but if thou art to be my new wife and run a tight ship, I pray take this opportunity to espouse to thee the virtues of accounting. My advice to any Lady of the House is to account for everything. Log every single item, every transaction, every purchase, every sale. Income and expenditure: balanced books for a balanced mind. It is a question of symmetry, in the Classical tradition. Know that symmetry is the expression of divine harmony and reveals God's hand in everything.

When Henry VIII died earlier this year, he left this country on the edge of bankruptcy; but as Treasurer of the King's Chamber, mine own person is in profit. Why? Because Good King Henry never understood the importance of numbers. It is my firm belief that all things in God's kingdom hath a mathematical framework. The hour is calculated by the sun's position in the sky. God created the world in seven days. Numbers are the music of the spheres. So too doth words have numerical value – as Chaucer understands only too well. Hath thy reading yet extended to Chaucer? No? Allow me to enlighten. Take this gift of his poems, "The Legend of Good Women". Thou wilt find much in it to please, not least "Penelope's Tale" of the virtues of loyalty and patience. Hast thou yet experienced the theatre? No? If it pleaseth, I will take thee to the "York Mysteries", where we shall witness the role of divine numbers in Creation.

It is said that good luck comes in pairs – like husband and wife. As such we shall enjoy a little gambling together. If one has a surplus of wealth, as indeed I do, then accounting can be very entertaining. One has to learn to hedge one's bets in this life. The fox knows that, to avoid the snare, he must not always use the one track. Observe how deftly I slide in my employ from one sovereign to another.

Know that Charity hath its place in the balance between rich and poor. Never give to the thriftless poor – the idle beggars, vagabonds, thieves, rogues and strumpets who wander from parish to parish, begging and stealing. Give instead to the "true poor" – those poor by impotence (the orphaned, the aged, blind and lame) and those poor by casualty (the wounded soldier, the diseased person). These must be provided for by the parish where they live.

In family matters, near half of all babies die within twelve months. There is need to plan for more births than required, if we are to build a substantial family life together.

Fear not, Good Bess, for I shall teach thee all things I know and thou wilt be a better person for it.

BESS: (*Aside*) Take heed, for this is what passeth for "wooing" in my day.

Cavendish disappears from screen.

There are two "confidantes" in my life – just as I am confidante to the two queens. Never hath I told anyone of this. It will not be found in any histories after I am gone. I give my confidantes secret names. They are both women: Mistress Pentecost and Mistress Petticoat.

Mistress Pentecost and Mistress Petticoat appear on screen when named. Both are played by Bess. Pentecost carries a bible, Petticoat carries a cat.

Mistress Pentecost is my priestess. She is my spiritual guide and helps me remain virtuous in a world of corruption and deceit.

Mistress Petticoat is my astrologer. She allows me to enjoy life in a world of entertainment and excitement.

They seldom agree on anything; but between them I hope to find some symmetry and balance to my life.

PETTICOAT: We are in favour of consulting the astrological charts to determine the best time to draw blood, to consider marriage prospects, the best time to set out on a journey, if your sailor husband will return, when to buy property, if a clergyman will be promoted, if a person is in love with you.

PENTECOST: We are against all attempts to tell the future from the stars. Or from dreams, except for those mentioned in the bible.

PETTICOAT: The Queen's horoscope was cast to divine the most auspicious date for her coronation.

PENTECOST: We are against the Queen – she is the illegitimate daughter of Anne Boleyn. We are in favour of the Queen's lover, the Earl of Leicester, for he is a Puritan sympathiser.

PETTICOAT: Francis Drake captained a ship all the way around the known world. The earth is proven round, There is talk that the earth orbits the sun and the stars are not fixed in the heavens.

PENTECOST: The earth is at the centre of God's universe. Mankind is at the centre of life on earth.

PETTICOAT: Spirits appear between the hours of midnight and cockcrow.

PENTECOST: We are in favour of prayer: in the morning, at dinner, in the evening and at bedtime; it is a crime not to attend church on Sundays and Holy Days. Remember, your servants are listening and watching.

PETTICOAT: It is possible to be a good Christian and a witch.

PENTECOST: We are against dancing, singing, playing the organ in church, theatre, maypoles, games, smoking, drinking, whoring and bear-baiting on a Sunday – on other days it is permissible.

PETTICOAT: For a good harvest, leave twelve corns for the twelve months of the year on a hot hearth. If a woman dreams of her lover presenting her with a swine's head as a gift, she shall forsake him. Do not lend fire to a neighbour or your horses will die. You can hurt a man by burning his excrement.

PENTECOST: We are against colourful clothes and foreign clothes, especially fashion: ruffs that make the head look like it is being served on a plate, silk stockings, breeches on boys under six years of age, unmarried women wearing doublets partially unbuttoned at the front to show cleavage, Venetian gowns, Polish black velvet gowns, Dutch black velvet gowns with Spanish sleeves, Spanish sleeves on French gowns with Dutch cloaks; white Spanish leather boots and high heels.

We are against make-up, except to cover pock-marks; we are against perfume, especially musk; and we are against mirrors – the devil could never have found a more pestilent evil than the looking-glass.

PETTICOAT: Mistress Pentecost, like most Puritans, has a bad word to say about everybody.

PENTECOST: It is faith in the Lord as allows a body to live virtuously in this world.

PETTICOAT: Aye, but 'tis money and title as allows a body to do as yer please.

PENTECOST: Fie for shame, Mistress Petticoat; lewd folk will take great heed and credence by thy wanton musings.

Mistress Penetecost and Mistress Petticoat disappear from screen. Music. Cavendish re-appears on screen.

BESS: (*To Audience*) Within a year of marriage,
I present my husband with a baby girl,
Frances, followed by Temperance who,
by God's will, doth not tarry long in this world.
Now I hath provided an heir
for the Cavendish name:
our first son, Henry, born
in the Boy King Edward's reign.

CAVENDISH: My old friend, Henry Grey, shall be Godfather.

43

BESS: This pleases me well, my Lord. And who shall be Godmother?

CAVENDISH: The Princess Elizabeth has agreed.

BESS: Who'd have thought? Henry VIII's daughter and my little Henry? A royal princess to christen our golden boy is the best start in life a mother could wish for.

CAVENDISH: There is more. I hath taken thy advice and purchased Chatsworth, at a bargain price. I shall instruct my master mason to design a fine new house for us.

BESS: I shall be your "builder" and see to it the work is of the highest standard.

CAVENDISH: I hath commissioned the finest blue livery for our staff, to demonstrate the high status of our household.

BESS: I shall furnish it with the finest tapestries.

CAVENDISH: I hath ordered us a bed, laced with pearls, and carved with the Cavendish coat of arms.

BESS: My Lord, I shall be thy most grateful mistress. (*Aside*) Can it be true? Am I to be Lady Cavendish of Chatsworth House? Imagine the scene: dozens of servants ready to serve my every whim – to fetch me a soothing draft of small beer during the day and a chamber pot at night. Servants everywhere, lying like dogs where they drop:

sleeping on kitchen floors, on landings, in corridors, curled up at the foot of my bed.

Chatsworth House.

BESS: (*To Audience*)
For nine days, England has two queens:
the Catholic Mary Tudor
and the Protestant Lady Jane Grey.
Mary seizes power
and Jane is held in the Tower
with her father, Lord Grey.
Far away, in the lush valleys of Derbyshire,
I am building us a home and a family
at Chatsworth, fit for royal visits.
Two more boys follow: William and Charles
while, at Court, their father lives by his wits.

(*To Cavendish*) It is indeed a royal coup to have Queen Mary as Godmother to our baby Charles; but to invite Lord Grey, fresh from the Tower on charges of treason, to be his Godfather? Hast thou lost thy wits, my Lord?

CAVENDISH: Lady Grey hath begged the Queen for Lord Grey's life and Her Majesty hath shown her mercy. All will be well. It will afford Lord Grey a chance to plead for Lady Jane's life. He is my dearest friend.

BESS: And none care more than I for poor Lady Jane; but thou knoweth it is to be a Catholic

45

christening – it can be nothing else in the presence of Her Majesty Queen Mary.

CAVENDISH: Our children's lives are worth a mass. Lord Grey has agreed. Thereby he can show his allegiance to the Queen.

BESS: When first I came to London, Lady Grey took me, one Sunday, to watch the bear-baiting in Southwark. For two pennies, we sat in the gallery while the bear was brought in chains into the arena and tied at the stake. A noble creature, with its pink eyes and huge paws, which could kill a man with one strike. Thereupon, a pack of great English Mastiffs was set upon the bear. For two pennies more, we bet on the game of life and death. As the dogs tore at its torso and throat, the bear would roar and shake its head of blood and saliva until the dogs tired or were killed. The bear was blindfolded while fresh dogs were unleashed to continue the assault until the bear was eventually exhausted. But because the bear was a valuable celebrity, it was not allowed to die.

CAVENDISH: Dost thou not know our superiority over the animal kingdom is granted to us by God? And doth not everyone love the thrill of power, money and chance?

Music.

BESS: (*To Audience*) Bloody Queen Mary is
infatuated still
with King Philip of Spain and is raising
money again to fund his wars.
There is much talk of the Inquisition
arriving on our shores.
Neighbours are baiting neighbours:
hatred turns to grief
as hundreds of men and women
are burned alive for their beliefs.
A celebrity scaffold is prepared:
a blindfolded Lady Jane bears herself
towards the block, in public view,
crying out to her executioner,
"What must I do?"
The axe falls once,
the axe falls twice,
before her headlong roll, like a dice
into the crowd who roar and chant
in a game of power, money and chance.
Princess Elizabeth is taken
to the Tower and baited with questions
for the next eight weeks,
knowing that she might suffer the same fate.
The public must be satisfied,
but with no evidence, Mary agrees
her sister Elizabeth will not be tried.
England is drawn, eventually,
into the Spanish war with France
and the Crown is in desperate need of money.

Cavendish writes to Bess.

47

CAVENDISH: "Good Bess, thou must come to London at once. The Privy Council hath audited our accounts."

BESS: "How so? There is not a single penny I hath not listed, just as thou taught me."

CAVENDISH: "It is not you, mine own dear wife; it relates to the time under good King Henry when I was charged with taking property and lands from the monasteries. I am called before the Star Chamber to account for my apparent debt to the Crown."

BESS: "I will leave baby Lucretia with the wet nurse and make haste with a small retinue. I shall be with thee in three days and three nights."

CAVENDISH: "Godspeed."

BESS: "Write to Her Majesty, she will not desert us."

CAVENDISH: "I, Sir William Cavendish, most humbly beseech Your Royal Majesty to pardon all things whereof I am most untruly deceived. Unto Her Majesty's merciful consideration I most humbly submit myself. Without a royal intercession, my good wife and I and our innocent children are utterly undone and like to end our days in no small penurie."

Cavendish disappears from screen.

BESS: (*To Audience*) Twelve days after the Hearing,
my beloved William is dead.
Our baby Lucretia, by God's will,
hath also from this world departed.
Family is everything to me:
I am age thirty with six small children and,
yet agen, I find mesen forced to the courts.
William's debt does not die with him,
so I can't afford to dwell on regrets.
If a woman is to truly serve
her family in this world,
she must first learn to serve hersen.

Music.

Mistress Petticoat re-appears on screen, with her cat.

PETTICOAT: My Lady Cavendish, henceforth thou shalt be known as "Bess the Builder" of grand and stately homes; but be warned, the greymalkin hath spoken: the prophecy states, "When the last stone is laid and the building stops, so Bess the Builder will be at rest."

INTERVAL.

FIVE: MASQUERADE

1559 - 1565. Bess aged 32 - 38.

Music. Bess is at a masqued ball at court.

BESS: (*To Audience*) At the modern masquerade, one is to appear suitably attired. One will find historical characters – over there I spyeth a Cleopatra – and Classical gods and goddesses – over there are Zeus and Venus. There are queens and maidens and fantastical creatures with wings, horns or tails; there are blackamoors – I am reliably informed it is increasingly fashionable to have one's own black servant (Her Majesty has blackamoor dancers and musicians for her entertainment).

I myself am dressed as a foreigner – normally one should avoid all things foreign, except for fashion. I hath a ruff around my neck and ruffles around my wrists; I hath Spanish leather boots, well-heeled in the modern style; my face is fashionably pale to attract the eye and I am wearing a little musk to attract the nose; my doublet is partially unbuttoned, showing cleavage to attract the male. There is indeed one particular medieval knight who seems to hath noticed my display.

There is a procession of costumes in front of painted scenery, with torches to illuminate our displays. Actors engage us in short dramatic exchanges of a witty nature. The music leads us into dance: firstly the "basse dance", which is gentle and reserved; followed by the "haute dance", which is energetic and allows a gentleman to display his moves and high-kicks. Her Majesty's favourite is the "galliard", which helps keep her fit and active. A lady is permitted to ask a gentleman to dance and it is bad manners to refuse; so I bide my time and wait for an opportunity to strut across the dance-floor and invite my medieval knight to accompany me.

St.Loe appears on screen.

He is a tall gentleman, in excellent shape; by all accounts in his prime. He sports a fashionable moustache and short pointed beard. He is indeed a great stag of a man. I wonder what great horn lies in wait beneath that codpiece? His presentation suggests a sense of humour – his attempts at high-kicks in body-armour draw much gaiety and laughter.

At the banquet, my knight in shining armour presents me with a gift: it is a "bone grace" – a velvet-covered ornament for the hair in the new fashion. Mmm, clearly a man of good taste. We exchange conversation over a final course of sweetmeats, an exotic root called "potato" and marzipan confections shaped like animals. My knight sups claret in a gold cup, whilst I sup white wine from La Rochelle. He tells me of his lands in Somerset and Gloucestershire. I speaketh a little of my beloved Derbyshire and am surprised when he refers to me as his "honest and sweet Chatsworth". I can only assume he suspects my identity.

At the close of the banquet, one removes one's masque to reveal with whom one has enjoyed the dance, the dining and the discourse. I recognise my knight instantly. At Her Majesty's Coronation earlier in the year, I remember him standing guard, in Westminster Abbey, over the dais on which the throne was placed. I recall his scarlet and black uniform, his hip-length cloak and the jaunty feather in his hat. He sayeth, he too noticed me, in the seating area for invited guests, and confesses his knowledge of me as Lady Cavendish, widowed of late. Sir William St.Loe is Captain of the Queen's Guard – a gallant knight indeed.

ST. LOE: (*To Audience*) In these modern times, the whole world is within reach. One can sail to the West Indies and home again in less than twelve weeks. But there is still no place like England. There are no vessels in the world compare to ours. We have in England great plenty of sundry minerals and metals: coal,

tin and lead mines, iron, quicksilver and
sulphur, sallpetre for our ordinance, salt soda
for our glass. There is no country that may
compare with ours in number, excellency
and diversity of dogs. The milk of our goats
is next in estimation to that of woman. With
God's blessing, this island is void of savage
beasts, such that our countrymen, herds and
flocks travel in safety. No nation under the
sun is more plentiful of wild and tame fowl.
Where other than this fertile land are oxen
made more large of bone, cows more
commodious for the pail, sheep more
profitable for wool and swine more
wholesome of flesh than here with us in
England?

Where else than in England might I find a
woman like Bess, with her bold equine face
and so fleet of foot on the dance-floor?

I shower her with gifts of oranges and
lemons, olives and cucumbers, pairs of
quartered velvet shoes, pairs of Spanish
gloves, black lace points and Spanish silks,
frankincense, wires for her virginals and a
knocker for the great gate at Chatsworth.

I love the way she talks away from Court:

"Av I eck as like"

"Woya born in a barn?"

"I'm reight pigged off"

"Mek do and mend"

"'Old yer 'osses!"

She is the finest Derbyshire mare, from those bleak hills where the heat of their stomach is greater.

BESS: (*To Audience*) True love never wears a mask when lovers' roles are cast.
Within the year we are betrothed.
Her Majesty approves the oaths,
sets a date for the marriage
and duly attends in her royal carriage.

(*To St.Loe*) My Captain, Her Majesty truly honours thy new wife. As our wedding gift, Her Royal Highness, this day, hath made me Lady of her Privy Chamber.

(*To Audience*) I attend to Her Majesty's person;
she is fastidious in her ablutions.
As I told the Venetian Ambassador
while we were dancing the gavotte:
"The Queen bathes every month,
whether she needs it or not."
These are intimate times, of course,
not least because of Her Majesty's love
for the Earl of Leicester, Master of the Horse.
There is much gossip and scandal

about the need for him to divorce.

(*To St.Loe*) I tell Her Majesty, "I have known Leicester since a youth, Your Grace, but I know him not as a man."

She says, "One should allow a man to be a man – how say you, my lady?"

"I can assure Your Majesty, my Captain is certainly "Master of *his* Horse".

She says, "St. Loe is a tall gentleman, we imagine he rides high in the saddle?"

"Indeed, I like it so, Your Grace."

"If only Leicester rode with such command of horse. We should like to see him ride bareback on occasion. At times, we suspect he would rather ride side-saddle."

"I've heard tell, Your Majesty, there are those who rather enjoy a man in touch with womanly ways."

"The bedchamber is not to be mistaken for the throne room. We like our men to know the difference."

Imagine, Her Majesty talking to me like we were two ale-house women, as thick as thieves.

(*To Audience*) Her Majesty doth seldom enjoy the sport of women;

methinks I hath achieved a special place at Court.
Leicester's wife is not so fortunate:
she is found by servants in a stairwell,
her neck broken, truth to tell.
The tragedy is forever left unspoken.

Music.

Mistress Pentecost and Mistress Petticoat appear on screen

PENTECOST: Ladies must never reveal their bare arms or legs in public, unless they are to be considered as washerwomen.

PETTICOAT: A woman is allowed no position of power other than churchwarden and yet the Queen is a woman?

PENTECOST: A single woman can travel, write, go about her daily business and pray as freely as any man.

PETTICOAT: A married woman's property is her husband's. She is allowed no business of her own.

PENTECOST: A married woman is, at least, an improvement on being a father's daughter. A husband is responsible for his wife's debts.

PETTICOAT: A man may legally beat an outlaw, a traitor, a pagan, a servant or a wife.

PENTECOST: Women are said to have more freedom in England than elsewhere in Europe. They say

England is a paradise for women, a prison for servants and a hell for horses.

PETTICOAT: If you kill your master, a man will be hanged; a woman will be burnt at the stake.

PENTECOST: Women can avoid execution by "pleading their belly".

PETTICOAT: It is accepted that the master of the house will have sex with his female servants. To refuse him is to risk losing your job; to submit is to risk disease and pregnancy, which will also lead to dismissal.

PENTECOST: Nine of every ten people who practise witchcraft are women.

PETTICOAT: I wonder why?

PENTECOST: How can women be equal to men when no two men are equal?

Petticoat and Pentecost disappear from screen. St.Loe re-appears. Music.

BESS: (*To Audience*) Will is an open-handed man
who gives alms to the poor,
to old soldiers he passes on the road
and tips to maids and porters.
He settles the Cavendish debt for me
and channels my sons through Eton;
he gives me funding and permission
to continue the Chatsworth extensions
and, in his will, makes me and mine heirs

his sole beneficiary.
But when his brother Edward
visits us in London, both Will
and I fall seriously ill.

(*To St.Loe*) The good doctor states, had not his remedy been swiftly applied, we both should have died.

ST.LOE: But who would have us poisoned?

BESS: Was not thy brother Edward's young wife poisoned?

ST.LOE: What of it? There is no evidence to suggest that Edward –

BESS: Listen to thine own mother who warns he likes nothing of our marriage. She has written to me, accusing her own son of being a poisoner.

ST.LOE: Can it be true?

BESS: He wears the guise of sibling as a mask, but reveals the true face of a sorcerer when he accuses me of trying to murder mine own husband.

ST.LOE: Godstruth, I will suffer none such slander of mine own sweet wife, who is more dearer to me than I am to myself.

BESS: Look to your brother that he doth not visit us again.

(*To Audience*) But dearest Will doth look
away:
whilst I am at Chatsworth, in London
he allows his brother Edward to stay once
more.
Unexpected news arrives at my door:
my husband hath taken suddenly ill.
I fail to return in time and Will dies
with Edward at his bedside.
I cannot prove the glass of water
given by Edward to my husband
was the cause of his slaughter,
but I can prove, in court, that papers signed
by Will, on his deathbed, are a lie.
We played well our lovers' roles,
but our dance of souls has ended:
Sir William St.Loe is dead.

Music.

The masque ends.

SIX: MAD DOG TALBOT

1580 – 1586. Bess aged 53 - 59.

Shrewsbury appears on screen. Bess and Shrewsbury are not speaking to each other. They address each other via the audience.

BESS: A "talbot" is the name given to a bloodhound, often tied to the back of a coach and horses.

SHREWSBURY: 'Tis a common jest there is but one "shrew" in all the world and every man hath her.

BESS: If "shrewness" be just cause for separation between man and wife, methinks very few men of England would keep their wives long.

SHREWSBURY: Thanks for the fat capon. I send with this letter a pheasant cock.

BESS: I opened your letter by mistake, thinking it for me.

SHREWSBURY: She is extravagant in her building and buying of lands to enrich her children. She constantly asks me for money.

BESS: He sides openly with his royal prisoner against his wife, humiliating me in front of servants.

SHREWSBURY: Bess knows the Scottish Queen better than any other woman, which makes her a most desirable guest at any dinner-party, to her own advantage.

BESS: She cannot do ill while she is with my husband and I begin to grow jealous, they are so great together.

SHREWSBURY: Her dutifulness and humility is but a siren's song; she seeks to spoil my goods by unnatural means and malice.

BESS: Do let me know how thou and thy charge are enjoying the waters at Buxton? I send with this letter some lettuce.

SHREWSBURY: I am over-run by my malicious wife. A man of my cut, ruled by a woman of so base a parentage.

BESS: I am better pleased by thine absence than by thy presence.

SHREWSBURY: She hath a wicked tongue. She threatens she knows things about me that would cause harm, if she were to make them public.

BESS: God forbid I should use any such speeches against him.

SHREWSBURY: I have been too bold with herring, which hath made me sick.

BESS: I have great need of a plumber.

SHREWSBURY: Thy messages show thy love for me hath gone; thou show thyself not to owe me any further obedience or duty.

BESS: He hath used me strangely in many things, in such sort as were enough to alienate the heart and duty of any wife.

SHREWSBURY: She hath turned mine own son Gilbert against me.

BESS: For thirty years I hath built and furnished my home at Chatsworth, only for him to prevent my living there. The "mad dog" arrives with forty armed men, forcing my son William to flee.

SHREWSBURY: Thou wert defamed, and to the world a byword, as St.Loe's widow. I covered those imperfections by my marriage with thee and brought thee to all the honour thou hast and to the most part of that wealth thou now enjoyst.

BESS: I hear a rumour that gout hath finally killed my husband. Would that it were so.

SHREWSBURY: It reaches the ears of Her Majesty that the Scottish Queen hath conceived my child. After fifteen years of safe-keeping, at mine own expense, the Queen finally removes her from my custody. I thank Her Majesty for delivering me from two she-devils – the Scottish Queen and my wife.

BESS: I am dragged before the Privy Council to answer charges of being the source of this rumour.

SHREWSBURY: Wife. The offences and faults thou hast committed against me, no good wife would do. There cannot be any wife more forgetful of her duty and less careful to please her husband than thou hast been. Thine insatiable greedy appetite doth betray thee.

BESS: Husband. As God is my witness, my heart thirsts after thy prosperity and desires nothing so much as thy love. How I deserve thy indignation is invisible to me? I beseech thee to give me liberty to come unto thee.

SHREWSBURY: Written at the suggestion of some smart lawyer, no doubt.

BESS: I am exonerated of all charges. The Queen refers to Shrewsbury as "disquieted, especially in the mind". Her Majesty hath ordered, by royal decree, that he must allow his wife to come unto him and to occupy and enjoy their properties.

SHREWSBURY: Her Majesty refers to me as her "good old man" and provides for me a footstool by her throne. She treats me as her lap-dog who fetches the stick to beat me with.

BESS: He hath truly put the "mad dog" in Talbot.

SHREWSBURY: She hath truly put the "shrew" in Shrewsbury.

Music.

SEVEN: THE EXECUTION

1587. Bess aged 60.

Music underscore. Fotheringhay Castle. Shrewsbury appears on screen.

SHREWSBURY: All around is madness. I am forced by our crazed Queen to oversee this execution. Why me? Hath I not suffered enough to please the Queen? For fifteen years I cared for this woman at mine own expense. For what? For her to kneel and rest her head on the chopping block like some common criminal?

BESS: What in hell's name possessed this Scottish Queen to put her signature to young Babbington's disastrous plot?

SHREWSBURY: I am forced to deliver to her face, at Fotheringhay Castle, the news of her execution. My voice falters as I read out the charges of attempting to facilitate the invasion of the realm and the destruction of the Queen's person, for which she is sentenced to death at eight o'clock the following morning. She says her "crime" is her loyalty to her Catholic faith and her claim to the English throne. Her concern is for her servants who hath shown her such loyalty.

BESS: There was a time I promised Mary, if her life was in danger, I would help her escape.

SHREWSBURY: I am forced to be the official witness for the Crown and to attend the proceedings. I sit on my stool at one end of the square platform. Mary enters and smiles at me on her approach, saying that she is ready to die. This legendary beauty, a plump and middle-aged woman, lame in one leg from rheumatism, retains an air of majesty. She is dressed in red, the colour of martyrdom; her rosary beads around her wrist, a cross in one hand and a Latin bible in the other. Her last request is that her ladies assist her to disrobe. I am concerned they might cry out and disrupt proceedings or dip their handkerchiefs in her blood as mementoes. She gives me her solemn word they will do neither, so I acquiesce. Her wit sharpens as she disrobes, saying how she hath never before taken off her clothes in such company. As she is blindfolded like an animal, she commends her spirit to the Lord and whispers, "In my end is my beginning."

I am forced to signal to the executioner when to strike. The first blow slices into her neck and causes her to moan in prayer. The second blow leaves the head hanging until a meat cleaver severs the bone. As the head is held aloft, it slips out of her wig and onto the floor, amidst cries of, "Such be the end of all the Queen's enemies and all the Gospel's enemies." I cannot speak; not even an

"Amen". Tears rip down my cheeks like stitches into cloth.

BESS: The Queen rages hysterically at the news of Mary's death, weeping and ranting as if some tragic accident hath occurred, not of her making.

SHREWSBURY: I am ordered to Court like all those involved in Mary's execution. But this is not why I have been summoned. The Queen wants to discuss my marriage. She orders me to live with my wife and binds me over to keep to the agreement or pay a fine of £40,000.

BESS: We remain together for a while at Wingfield Manor, aware that we are being watched. The Queen's attention is consumed by the Spanish Armada threatening our shores. I slip away to spend my time at Hardwick with my grandchild, Arbella. Hardwick and Arbell are both in need of constant attention, if I am to become a maker of queens. With Mary gone, Arbell is second in line to the throne.

SHREWSBURY: I offer my services to the Queen: "I am old, your Grace, but the Queen's quarrel with Spain will make me young again. I am lusty in heart to lend your greatest enemy one final blow and die in your service."

BESS: In truth, "mad dog" is busy servicing his housekeeper, Mistress Britton, on whom he dotes until the end of his years.

Music.

EIGHT: PALACE OF SYMMETRY

1597. Bess aged 70. Hardwick Hall.

BESS: (*To Arbella*) £6360 spent on our parade at court and still nothing hath been decided of thy future. The old guard is gone; only Burghley's son favours thee as successor. We are taken for the Queen's Fool.

Our hope lies in a solitary letter from King James of Scotland, at last acknowledging thy close kinship – "the strict band of nature and blood, whereby we are linked." Better that he should return the Lennox jewels to thee, their rightful owner, but a letter, at least, is hope for thy future.

'Tis time to move on. I care not if the New Hall is not yet finished, we will move in. If there is no water for the mortar, let them use beer. I will wait no longer. I am fast approaching my 70th year. Though I be balanced on this stick with rheumatics, we shall hold court and entertain. We hath created a small village supplying us with milk and cheese, butter and cream, meat and fish, fruit and veg, beer and bread, honey and herbs, medicines and wool, water and flowers. 74 servants are in our employ.

375 local craftsmen and labourers have built this great hall, with local minerals: timber, sandstone, limestone, lead and iron,

alabaster, black marble and glass. The men hath done the crafting, but 'tis the local women hath been their labourers, at a penny a day. During the famine years, when the price of bread went through the roof, I tripled their wages to three pennies per day, that they should not have to labour on empty stomachs.

Bess walks with her stick to the new hall at Hardwick.

(*To Audience*) According to Mistress Petticoat's prophecy,
when the lady stops her building,
then shall she die.
So the building will never stop;
this prophecy I shall deny.
Finally, I have balance in my life:
this is my palace of symmetry,
of the regal and ethereal,
a building of great height and mystery;
it is a cathedral of light,
catching the setting sun,
filled with great tapestries;
a statement of wealth and grace,
in the modern style of the Renaissance,
with six great towers,
crowned with huge stone initials:
"E.S." - Countess Elizabeth Shrewsbury -
more "shrewd" than "shrew".
a testament to my power and glory.

Music. Party.

Essex is here, which should keep Arbell happy, flirting with a national hero. Poor Arbell, she still deems unrequited love more important than unrequited sovereignty.

While plague rages in London, The Queen's Players are here, performing an history of Henry VI, at my request. The hero of the tale is one Lord John Talbot, the First Earl of Shrewsbury. Another national hero, by all accounts, who defeated the French almost single-handedly. The last of the medieval knights, they say his tale marks the end of the age of chivalry. Clearly the writer cannot have met my Captain St.Loe.

If this young Shakespeare hath my skill as a diplomat, he might yet make a name for himself. What, I wonder, would the "valiant Lord Talbot" have made of my initials commanding the Derbyshire skyline?

Shrewsbury appears on the screen.

SHREWSBURY: (*As Shakespeare's John Talbot*) "No, I am but a shadow of myself.

You are deceiv'd, my substance is not here;
For what you see is but the smallest part
And least proportion of humanity.
I tell you, madam, were the whole frame here,
It is of such a spacious lofty pitch
Your roof were not sufficient to contain it."

BESS: George? Is this some trick of Shakespeare's that likens my "mad dog" to the valiant John Talbot?

SHREWSBURY: (*To audience*) Good wife Bess, she likes everything to be in balance. No time for the unstable, cockeyed, unnatural, lopsided, irregular rantings of an old man with a disquieted mind.

BESS: What is up wi' yo? Thou art dead at this point in the story. I hath not called upon thee to testify. Be gone!

SHREWSBURY: (*To Bess*) There is need of someone to tell how things art really in thy palace of symmetry. Arbella is kept a virtual prisoner in thine house. She is made to sleep in thy chamber and not allowed to leave the grounds. As we kept the Scottish Queen, so too doth thou shackle this young princess.

BESS: She is free to go at any time.

SHREWSBURY: Aye, but not to marry.

BESS: My grand-daughter shall one day be Queen of England.

SHREWSBURY: Never wilt thou place her on the throne. She will wither on the vine like ripened fruit which never hath been plucked.

BESS: Be gone, I say, dark shadow of thy former self!

Shrewsbury disappears.

Music. Bess is embroidering with Arbella.

> (*To Arbella*) Sit with me, Arbell, and sew, as once I sat with mine own mother. The trick is to find a way to manage the tension in the frame. Embroidery is a skill conveying a woman's rank and social standing. Look for guidance to the tapestries of the "virtuous women" in the High Great Chamber. Let me tell thee of "Penelope's Tale". See how the faithful and patient wife of Ulysses waits for her husband to return from the Trojan Wars. She refuses to re-marry or take a lover until she finishes weaving his burial shroud. By day, she weaves. By night, she secretly unpicks the weave. For twenty years, Penelope weaves the same shroud until, finally, her patience and perseverance are rewarded by her husband's return.

Music.

NINE: VIRTUE

1600. Bess aged 73.

Bess is praying. Mistress Pentecost appears on screen.

BESS: The New Hall at Hardwick is done
but the building work must go on.
Mistress Pentecost, what am I to do?
How am I to maintain mine own virtue?

PENTECOST: Pray to God in your chapel every day;
give alms to the poor who wait
every week at your gates.
Build almshouses for the elderly:
respite for twelve people until they die;
give each an annual stipend.

BESS: Yes, and each a suit of clothes bearing my crest
and the initials "E.S.".

PENTECOST: At the Church of All Hallows in Derby,
build a vault for your family;
have teams of horses drag forty
loads of stone from local quarries.

BESS: And in this room, I shall instruct
my designer, Robert Smythso,
to make me a marble tomb,
topped with a life-size effigy
of me at prayer and laid to rest
so people shall know, for all time,
in God's house am I blessed.

PENTECOST: Your funeral shall not be over-sumptious
but will reflect your status.
Your life will be celebrated,
but the expenses carefully calculated.

Mistress Petticoat appears on screen.

PETTICOAT: And while "the Queen of Hardwick" lies in
state,
her servants will be home alone –
the big house all to themselves for one night
only.
Imagine the scene as servants, squirming
on the floor, rise up like serpents, slithering
across banqueting tables, sitting
on thrones and climbing into beds, rolling
themselves up in bed-linen and tapestries,
role-playing their mistress,
with chamber-pots on their heads
and cod-pieces in their mouths
in an orgy of "release",
where fun and fornication
overthrows status and nation.

Music.

74

TEN: DISINHERITANCE

1602. Bess aged 75.

BESS:

(*To Arbella*) What, in God's name, wert thou thinking? A Royal Commissioner, sent by the Queen hersen, coming here to Hardwick to investigate! Edward Seymour is of the royal blood of Henry VII and, like thee, stupid girl, hath claim to the throne. Hast thou lost thy wits, wench? This is thy choice of husband? A seventeen year old youth? Thou art near ten years his senior. Have I not oft-times told thee of the fate of the Grey sisters? Yet still thou thinks it reight to approach their family? When wilt thou get it into thy thick head that thy marriage is a matter of state business, by order of the Queen? After everything I hath done to find thee a husband. Thou thankless child, I should strike thee down!

To ask the Seymour family to come to Hardwick, my home, in disguise, to "free" thee from thy luxurious "bondage"? Wilt thou offer the Queen all our heads as traitors? Like thy reckless popinjay Essex?

Write down thy confession. Have it ready for the Commissioner upon his arrival. Take responsibility for thine own destruction. Do not smear our good family name. I shall write to the Queen.

Bess drafts a letter, ending:

"Your Most Royal Highness, the bad persuasions of some have so estranged Arbella's mind and natural affection for me that she holds me her greatest enemy. I most humbly beseech your Majesty that she may be placed elsewhere, to learn to be more considerate, and that after, it may please your Majesty either to accept her service about your royal person, or to bestow her in marriage, which in all humility and duty, I do crave your Majesty."

(*Aside*) My little jewel plots once more to break the Queen's wish that she remain at Hardwick. My own bad son Henry plots with her. Can they not see that Her Majesty suspects them of trying to seize the crown? Never hath I sought to endanger the sovereign realm. Neither will I now, in these, my final years.

Why, when our children and grand-children are born into greater advantage, can they not accomplish as much? Or, at the very least, capitalise on their good fortune?

The time has come for me to disinherit those from my will, who will not help themselves.

ELEVEN: END OF AN ERA

1603. Bess aged 76.

Music. St.Loe appears on screen.

BESS: The Thames hath frozen over. The Queen lies in state on a black velvet bed. No longer will I dream of receiving the Queen to my High Great Chamber, with its throne of silk and gold.

ST.LOE: In death, as in life, Her Royal Highness wants her people to see her.

BESS: My Captain, it puts me in mind of her glorious coronation.

ST.LOE: Thousands line the route. Her chariot is draped in black velvet. On top of the coffin is a wax effigy of Her Majesty. A dozen noblemen alongside, carrying banners depicting the lion of England, the dragon of Wales, the Tudor greyhound and the fleur-de-lis of France. A thousand invited mourners form a procession.

BESS: I am not sufficiently able-bodied to attend. Arbell refuses to go. As the closest living female relative, Arbell should be the Principal Mourner; but because she was denied an audience in the Queen's lifetime, she says she's not about to pay her an audience in death.

ST.LOE: Forty-five years our great Queen ruled, surviving eight assassination attempts and military coups. When she smiled, it was pure sunshine that everyone could bask in; but anon would come a terrible storm and thunder and lightning fall on all alike. She has died a virgin, without heirs, as she proclaimed at her coronation that she would. Truly, the Tudor line is at an end. It is Mary Stuart's line succeeds her. They say she uttered Mary's name at the last, in fear of divine justice for killing an anointed queen.

BESS: There was a day I heard my name from Her Majesty's own lips: "There is no lady in this land I better like and love than thee, my Lady Bess." As I heard upon a time my name from the lips of the Scottish Queen: "Had I been Bess' own queen, she could not have done more for me."

ST.LOE: It is the end of an era that, from this time forth, shall be known as "Elizabethan". The medieval hath given way to the modern.

BESS: I have outlived four monarchs and enter my fifth under King James, but I fear the fabric of my reign is beginning to unravel.

Music. St.Loe disappears from screen.

TWELVE: THE GODMOTHER AND THE KING

1603 -1606. Bess aged 76 - 79.

Cavendish appears on screen.

BESS: Arbell is gone, on the King's orders: (*reading a letter from the king*)

"We are desirous to free our cousin, the Lady Arbella, from that unpleasant life which she hath led in the house of her Grandmother, with whose severity and age, she – being a young lady – could hardly agree."

Not a word of thanks to her "severe grandmother" for the devotion and care lavished on her since birth. Furthermore, the King is to stay with Gilbert and Mary at Worksop. How so, with their poor finances? When I hath the Grand High Chamber at Hardwick, specifically designed for such a royal visit? No doubt, my son-in-law will come a-begging, cap-in-hand for a contribution.

CAVENDISH: Your daughter Mary is hosting the King. Your grand-daughter, Arbell, is favoured at Court. Is this not what you wanted for our family?

BESS: Fine. Let her take a prominent role in the coronation. And let the King pay Arbella's maintenance. Oh, how she shines in her element.

CAVENDISH: She is helping our son William gain a peerage.

BESS: Aye, whilst our eldest, Henry, is questioned over a plot to kill the King and place Arbell on the throne.

CAVENDISH: Arbell has not been questioned and Henry maintains his innocence.

BESS: Henry is deeply in debt and threatening to sell Chatsworth. He has produced no legitimate offspring, despite siring countless bastards in the county, bringing shame upon the family. I have written to Lord Burghley, the Younger, and told him I will not pay Henry's debts, nor will I plead his innocence. I have been so badly dealt with by Henry, that I must crave pardon if I refuse to do for those who have sought to hurt me. He is cut from my will, alongside Arbell.

I am in horror of their debts and casual attitude to money. Only our good son, William, harvests money as I hath done. I will not allow my inheritance to be frittered away by Arbell and our bad son, Henry.

CAVENDISH: Good wife Bess, look to thine own health for the final years.

BESS: I hath been ill some time and now the King hath written again that I should receive Arbell at Hardwick and, for his sake, treat her kindly. I hath told the King, I find it very strange that Arbell wants to visit Hardwick when she was forever keen to leave it. I told him my grand-daughter would always find a welcome at Hardwick, but that there are other grandchildren of mine in greater need of my bounty.

CAVENDISH: Our other grand-daughters have all married well and are happy.

BESS: 'Tis true that Gilbert and Mary's youngest, Alathea, hath dutifully conceived of a great grandson, named after the King, who has agreed to stand as Godfather to the child – for the first time I might add. I am to be Godmother, standing shoulder to shoulder with the King.

Unfortunately, when it comes to the day, I am ill and Arbell stands in for me.

CAVENDISH: This is the family we created, Bess, for better or worse.

Cavendish disappears from screen.

Music.

81

THIRTEEN: LEGACY

1608. Bess aged 81.

Bess is dictating her last requests to her son, William. Her mind swings from lucid to demented. Cavendish, St.Loe and Shrewsbury appear on screen together. Each, in turn, sheds a tear for Bess.

BESS: My good son William, thou art my sole executor. I entrust thee to continue my life's work. Write down all I say. Mary and Gilbert are allowed to visit. And Charles. But do not leave me alone with them, lest I should say something I regret.

There's a gift for thy son Wylkyn of £2000, for he is marrying sensible and well.

She takes up a bowl of broth but suddenly puts it down again.

Hath the water for this broth been fetched from the well? I fear 'tis poisoned.

My bad son Henry is to receive not a single mark. Arbell shall receive £300 and a gold cup.

Where is my holey stone? I need it to see into the afterlife.

My mind rages with my affairs, there's so much still to do.

How old am I? No person seems to know how old am I?

Mrs Digby hath been at my side day and night, these past days – see to it Goodwife Digby receives £100 cash. I have £1000 here to be divided 'mongst those servants who hath served me well.

Make sure my Lord Talbot is kept indoors, 'tis not fit to turn a dog out. Fetch me the Captain's saddle – St.Loe is to ride again this night. Tell Cavendish, there is no number for death but infinity. Sweet Robert, my little lamb, come to my bed and I will make a man of thee.

Cavendish, St.Loe and Shrewsbury fade from screen.

Dr Hunton hath given me treacle for my cough and hot plasters to encourage sweating.

See to the tapestries. "The Virtuous Women" are to carry me to church. I shall be rolled up in "Penelope's Tale". Fetch me a needle – I shall sew mine own eyes in readiness for death.

They say, in London the smell of dead bodies foul the streets.

The Scottish Queen was a murderer.
The Virgin Queen was a boy.
The Commoner Queen was a nobody,
with a nothing life to enjoy.

I hear Arbell is clothed in silks and jewels and dances "The Masque of Beauty" before the King.

She'll come a cropper, that one.

On screen the Arbella doll comes alive and dances and sings.

ARBELLA: *Some Queens shine and some Queens fade,*
some Queens are born and some Queens made.
Howl, howl, the hyenas howl
and gather at Hardwick's gates;
foul, foul, the relatives foul
and ravage the Queen's estate.
Some Queens shine and some Queens fade,
some Queens are born and some Queens made.

BESS: Upon my death, Dr. Hunton is to receive 40
marks – mind the amount, I desire it to be
exact. 40 marks saw me into this world and
40 marks shall see me out.

I must have symmetry.

Mistress Petticoat appears on screen.

BESS: My epitaph will say,
"she built magnificent buildings",
and yet I find that building is not so hard:
one brick on another like a house of cards;
but a legacy?
A legacy is not of brick but blood
and cannot readily be understood.
Mistress Petticoat, consult thy oracle
and foretell how my deeds will be noted?

PETTICOAT: A mighty river is made from humble
streams:
thou shalt beget queens,

84

though thou be none.
Understand this: there will come a time
when a second Elizabeth rules this land
and she will be of thy bloodline.

BESS: Everyone casts a shadow in the sun:
we all hath good and bad deeds done.

END.